W9-BYH-103

THE LOST CIVILIZATION OF
ATLANTIS

Don Nardo

ReferencePoint Press

San Diego, CA

About the Author

Historian and award-winning author Don Nardo has written numerous books about the ancient world, its peoples, their cultures, and their mythologies, including volumes on the Sumerians, Babylonians, Assyrians, Persians, Greeks, Etruscans, Romans, and others. He has also published single-volume encyclopedias on the ancient Mesopotamian, Greek, and Roman civilizations. Nardo, who also composes and arranges orchestral music, lives with his wife, Christine, in Massachusetts.

© 2020 ReferencePoint Press, Inc.
Printed in the United States

For more information, contact:
ReferencePoint Press, Inc.
PO Box 27779
San Diego, CA 92198
www.ReferencePointPress.com

ALL RIGHTS RESERVED.
No part of this work covered by the copyright hereon may be reproduced or used in any form or by any means—graphic, electronic, or mechanical, including photocopying, recording, taping, web distribution, or information storage retrieval systems—without the written permission of the publisher.

LIBRARY OF CONGRESS CATALOGING-IN-PUBLICATION DATA

Name: Nardo, Don, 1947– author.
Title: The Lost Civilization of Atlantis/by Don Nardo.
Description: San Diego, CA: ReferencePoint Press, Inc., 2020. | Series:
    Historic Disasters and Mysteries | Audience: Grades: 9 to 12. | Includes
    bibliographical references and index.
Identifiers: LCCN 2018058210 (print) | LCCN 2018061544 (ebook) | ISBN
    9781682826348 (eBook) | ISBN 9781682826331 (hardback)
Subjects: LCSH: Atlantis (Legendary place)
Classification: LCC GN751 (ebook) | LCC GN751 .N373 2020 (print) | DDC
    001.94—dc23
LC record available at https://lccn.loc.gov/2018058210

CONTENTS

Atlantis Removed from Fiction's Realm

"My excitement grew as we approached Thera for the first time, a dream coming true." With these words, James W. Mavor Jr., a marine engineer at the Woods Hole Oceanographic Institution in Massachusetts, recalled the daring 1966 expedition of the Woods Hole research vessel *Chain*. Standing on deck, Mavor and his fellow researchers silently stared with wonder as the ship entered the central bay of the Greek island of Santorini. Like many fellow scientists and historians, Mavor called the island by its ancient name, Thera. "Our excitement was intense," he later wrote. "At the entrance into the immense bay nearly vertical cliffs rose on both sides. It was the most awesome marinescape I had ever seen."[1]

Thera lies about 80 miles (129 km) north of the large island of Crete, not far from the center of the Aegean Sea's blue-green waters. The *Chain*'s mission was to investigate not only Thera and Crete but also other nearby Aegean islands. All of them had been affected by an ancient calamity—a tremendous Bronze Age eruption of the volcano situated at the center of Thera's bay. Still active today, it continues to erupt on occasion, although not nearly as violently as it did some thirty-six centuries ago.

Scientists had long known about the Theran volcano. They also knew that it had blown its top during the Bronze Age and that the towering cliffs surrounding the island's bay had formed during that long-ago catastrophe. What was new—and had inspired the *Chain*'s present voyage—was a possible link between the ancient eruption and one of history's most famous mysteries. In the middle to late 1960s, Mavor and his companions were only a few among a growing number of scientists and historians who suspected they could solve the long-standing riddle of Atlantis.

First described by the renowned classical Greek scholar Plato, Atlantis had traditionally been called a lost continent or lost civilization. Supposedly, it consisted of a powerful, culturally advanced island nation that had suddenly sunk into the sea, never to be seen again. Serious scholars had long assumed that both the ancient island and the disaster that

Did You Know?
The vertical cliffs lining Santorini's bay reach a height of 1,200 feet (366 m) in some places.

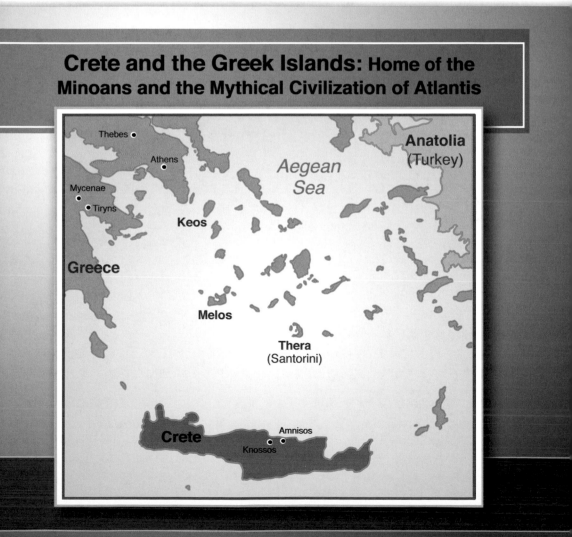

Crete and the Greek Islands: Home of the Minoans and the Mythical Civilization of Atlantis

Thebes

Athens

Mycenae

Tiryns

Keos

Greece

Melos

Thera
(Santorini)

Aegean
Sea

Anatolia
(Turkey)

Crete

Amnisos

Knossos

destroyed it were only myths. But in the past century archaeologists and other experts have found various pieces of evidence suggesting that Thera's monstrous ancient outburst may have been the one Plato had mentioned. Moreover, they conjectured, if the catastrophe indeed had been genuine, might Atlantis itself have been a real place? As Mavor put it in 1969,

> Atlantis, the greatest legend of the sea, has reverberated in people's minds for over 2,000 years and through the pages of as many volumes. The story, as told by Plato, has been given countless interpretations, all deriving from the assumption that somehow it masked a physically real and living place that had once, in truth, existed. [And] now, in support of that contention, modern science has found incontrovertible evidence of a real catastrophe worthy of Plato's description of the fantastic disappearance of Atlantis. [It is] a discovery that removes it from the realm of fiction and exaggeration and makes the facts of the story completely intelligible.[2]

Mavor and the other scholars knew that over the centuries writers of all kinds had speculated that Atlantis might have been a real place. Also, people had periodically searched for it in diverse locations all over the world. The most common assumption was that its remains must lie at the bottom of some sea or deep beneath centuries of built-up soil deposits. After all, Plato had described the lost continent sinking downward into oblivion.

Yet, Mavor and his colleagues reasoned, the idea that the ancient Theran eruption had destroyed the Atlantean civilization put a new spin on the search. Despite the enormous scope of the disaster, Crete still existed, as did parts of Thera itself. If these were, in fact, remnants of Atlantis, it meant that all those global pursuits of a sunken or buried civilization had been pointless. Mavor found himself struck by the profound realization that perhaps "Atlantis had lain exposed for centuries, for all to see, if they but knew what to look for."[3]

CHAPTER ONE

The Global Search for Atlantis

The first mention in Western literature of Atlantis came from the fertile mind and pen of the renowned fourth-century BCE Athenian scholar Plato. His description of that lost civilization appears in his dialogues the *Timaeus* and the *Critias*, written circa 355 BCE, when he was around seventy-two. In each of those works, as in his many other dialogues, several characters discuss a controversial political, historical, legal, or moral topic or issue. (More often than not, one of the speakers is Plato's old friend and mentor, the philosopher Socrates.)

A thriving island-based nation or empire, Plato stated, had existed in the Atlantic Ocean many centuries before his own time. Eventually, after fighting and losing a war with the early Athenians, he wrote, Atlantis was destroyed utterly by an enormous natural disaster. After Plato's passing, this basic Atlantean legend survived and became a favorite subject of writers around the world. Over time, the very name *Atlantis* emerged as a potent symbol of mystery and intrigue and seemed to acquire a life of its own. Indeed, remarks American marine biologist Richard Ellis, "it is a story so powerful that it has lasted solely on the basis of its own merits, passed along, often by word of mouth, for two and a half millennia, and today, in an era characterized by technological marvels like atomic energy and the Internet, the legend of Atlantis still thrives."[4]

In his writings, the ancient Greek philosopher Plato (pictured center with long gray beard), described a thriving island-based empire that had existed in the Atlantic Ocean centuries before his own time.

Driving and perpetuating this legend have been well over two thousand books and numerous scholarly articles, along with many short stories, novels, and movies. These sources have explored all manner of disasters to explain Atlantis's sudden disappearance. Moreover, they have placed it not only in the Atlantic Ocean, as Plato did, but also in dozens of other locations around the globe. In the words of the late Irish historian J.V. Luce, "Atlantis has been sought literally from Ceylon [Sri Lanka] to Mexico, and there are so many false trails that it is hard to know where to begin."[5]

Atlantis Sinks Again?

Attempts to place the lost continent in diverse locations actually did not begin until many centuries after Plato's time. In fact, most ancient scholars and writers who succeeded him assumed he had made up the story of Atlantis to illustrate some moral principle or lesson. Plato's famous student, Aristotle, for instance, was sure that his teacher had simply invented the tale. More than three hundred years later, the noted first-century CE Greek biographer and moralist Plutarch was of the same opinion. The story of the Atlantean civilization's demise was largely a literary fiction, he stated.

Plutarch flourished during the early years of the Roman Empire. Much later, shortly before that realm's collapse in the fifth century CE, a few Greek and Roman writers became the first to describe Atlantis as a real place. The fourth-century Roman historian Ammianus Marcellinus was one such writer. Another was the fifth-century Greek thinker Proclus, who wrote, "That [so] great an island once existed is evident by what is said by certain historians respecting what pertains to the external sea. For according to them, there were seven islands in that sea [and] also three others of immense extent, one of which was sacred to [the sea god] Poseidon [and] had domination over all the islands in the Atlantic."[6]

Proclus was one of the last ancient scholars who mentioned Atlantis. In contrast, writers in the ten medieval centuries that followed Rome's fall paid very little attention to the lost continent. Christian monks and medieval Europe's few other educated residents were far more interested in religious topics than historical stories. As a result, as one modern observer puts it, "Atlantis would seem to have sunk a second time." Except for a minor reference in an encyclopedia, "nothing more [was] heard of it for many centuries."[7]

Did You Know?
According to Plato's account, Atlantis was divided into ten mostly equal-sized sections.

Atlantis in the Americas?

This situation began to change in a big way after European explorers happened upon the Americas in the late 1400s and early 1500s. In 1553 Spanish scholar Francesco López de Gómara proposed a concept that appeared quite believable at the time. It was that the Americas as a whole were Plato's long-lost continent of Atlantis. The primary error Plato had made, López de Gómara pointed out, was saying that the landmass had collapsed into the sea since clearly the Americas were still very much intact.

In this excerpt from his famous 1882 book about Atlantis, Ignatius Donnelly offers an example of what he sees as the diffusion of Atlantean culture to both sides of the Atlantic—the cross symbol sacred to Christianity. Modern scholars point out that Donnelly makes it sound as if diffusion from Atlantis is the only viable explanation, completely ignoring that various peoples could have invented the cross symbol independently.

> When the Spanish missionaries first set foot upon the soil of America, in the fifteenth century, they were amazed to find the Cross was as devoutly worshipped by the red Indians as by themselves. [It] appeared on the bas-reliefs of ruined and deserted [palaces] as well as on those of inhabited palaces, and was the most conspicuous ornament in the great temple of Gozumel, off the coast of Yucatan. According to the particular locality, and the purpose which it served, it was formed of various materials—of marble and gypsum in the open spaces of cities and by the way-side; of wood in the teocallis, or chapels on pyramidal summits and in subterranean sanctuaries; and of emerald or jasper in the palaces of kings and nobles. When we ask the question how it comes that the sign of the Cross has thus been reverenced from the highest antiquity by the races of the Old and New Worlds, we learn that it is a reminiscence [cultural memory] of the Garden of Eden, in other words, of Atlantis.

Ignatius Donnelly, *Atlantis: The Antediluvian World*. 1882. Reprint, Scotts Valley, CA: CreateSpace, 2016, pp. 319–20.

A piece of evidence that seemed to support this theory was a legend held by the Aztecs, the leading native people of what is now Mexico. They claimed that their ancestors hailed from a place called Aztlan, which, López de Gómara said, sounded strangely similar to the name *Atlantis*. This theory retained widespread support from educated Europeans during the 1600s, partly because the popular English scholars John Swan and Francis Bacon accepted it.

Over time, however, the notion that the Americas and Atlantis were the same place steadily fell out of favor. This was primarily because it did not match up with certain other points Plato had made in his account. For example, he described Atlantis as having an advanced culture that created an empire incorporating much of Europe. Yet the Europeans who colonized the Americas during the 1600s and 1700s viewed the native inhabitants they encountered as inferior primitives. The colonists, therefore, concluded that the indigenous people of the Americas could never have possessed a large, technologically advanced navy capable of crossing the Atlantic and conquering Europe. Thus, the American continents must not have been Atlantis.

Atlantis—the Cradle of Civilization?

Could it be, some early modern European and American writers asked, that Plato's placement of Atlantis in the Atlantic Ocean had been correct all along? If that were the case, perhaps the Atlanteans had conquered or at least colonized lands on both sides of that great waterway. This thought-provoking concept became the main argument put forward by the most widely read and influential person (with the exception of Plato himself) ever to write about Atlantis. His name was Ignatius Donnelly. After running a small newspaper in Minnesota during the mid-1800s and serving in Congress for that state for a few years, he wrote *Atlantis: The Antediluvian World*, initially published in 1882. (*Antediluvian* means "before the great flood," or very ancient.)

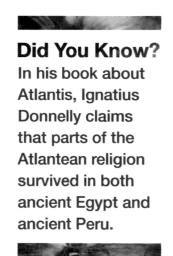

Did You Know?
In his book about Atlantis, Ignatius Donnelly claims that parts of the Atlantean religion survived in both ancient Egypt and ancient Peru.

A huge and complex work, Donnelly's book was, and remains (as it is still in print), a massive compilation of facts, cultural comparisons, historical suppositions, and out-and-out guesswork. All of this literary bluster attempts to support the theory that Atlantis was the original cradle of human civilization. Moreover, Donnelly held, all of humanity's positive traits were handed down from the "mother" society that arose in that wondrous but now lost continent. At one point in the book he briefly summarized his thesis, saying that the Atlanteans were the founders of nearly all our arts and sciences; they were the parents of our fundamental beliefs; they were the first civilizers, the first navigators, the first merchants, the first colonizers of the earth; their civilization was old when Egypt was young, and they had passed away thousands of years before Babylon, Rome, or London were dreamed of. [The Atlanteans'] blood flows in our veins; [and] every line of race and thought, of blood and belief, leads back to them.[8]

Donnelly went on to make many controversial claims about Atlantis, including that it was the Garden of Eden and Greece's Mount Olympus (home of the Greek gods). He claimed that the gods of Greece, Rome, and other European lands were actually the kings and queens of Atlantis, and the Atlantean language was the parent of all European tongues. Donnelly also alleged that all the flood legends in the world were distorted memories of the catastrophe that destroyed Atlantis.

Donnelly amassed an immense following of nonscholarly readers, many of whom looked on his book as a sort of new bible that explained all that was needed to know about humanity's origins. In contrast, scientists, archaeologists, and other scholars panned the work as a conglomeration of mostly unsupported and unproven conjecture. Donnelly was not a trained scientist, they pointed out, and he frequently displayed a lack of critical judgment. A close look at the book, popular historical writer L. Sprague de Camp states, reveals how careless, biased, "and generally worthless it is." Most of his supposed facts "either were wrong when he made them, or have been disproved by subsequent discoveries."[9]

From the Caribbean to Nigeria

In spite of the weaknesses of Donnelly's book, it spawned subsequent generations of writers who were sure that Atlantis was a real place and produced their own books and articles about it. Several used a newly coined word—*Atlantologist*—to describe themselves. Some continued to insist that Atlantis was a large

Numerous scholars, writers, and even psychics have speculated on the demise and true identity of Atlantis. Possible locations of the lost civilization have been placed across the globe.

island in the Atlantic Ocean. One of the best known, Scottish researcher Lewis Spence, published *The Problem of Atlantis* in 1924 and later wrote four other books on the subject. Spence insisted that there had been two massive islands in the Atlantic — Atlantis, situated near Europe, and Antillia, located closer to the Caribbean Sea. In fact, he claimed, the present-day Caribbean islands are the remnants of the mostly sunken Antillia.

As increasing numbers of books about Atlantis appeared over the decades, some self-proclaimed psychics saw a chance to cash in on the subject's growing popularity. Most famous among these was Kentucky native Edgar Cayce. In his so-called readings, often performed in large tent gatherings in the mid-1900s, he appeared to go into a trance, during which he recited large amounts of information about people and events in both the past and future. In many of his trances, and in books he published later, he claimed to have seen images of Atlantis in its heyday. The Atlanteans, he said, possessed airplanes, electricity, and other modern-style examples of advanced technology. Cayce also predicted that Atlantis would suddenly rise up from the ocean in

Atlantis in the North Sea?

The late renowned marine scientist Rachel Carson wrote briefly about Atlantis in her popular book *The Sea Around Us*, tentatively suggesting the lost continent might have been in the North Sea:

> Only a few scores of thousands of years ago, the [North Sea's] Dogger Bank was dry land, but now the fishermen drag their nets over this famed fishing ground, catching cod and hake and flounders among its drowned tree trunks. [Thousands of years ago], when immense quantities of water were withdrawn from the ocean and locked up in the glaciers, the floor of the North Sea emerged and for a time became land. It was a low, wet land, covered with peat bogs; then little by little the forests from the neighboring high lands [encroached]. Animals moved down from the mainland and became established on this land recently won from the sea. [Early humans] moved through the forests, carrying crude stone instruments; they stalked deer and other game. . . . Then as the glaciers began to retreat and floods from the melting ice poured into the sea and raised its level, this land became an island. Probably the men escaped to the mainland, [leaving] their stone implements behind. [Eventually] the sea covered the island, claiming the land and all its life. As for the men who escaped, perhaps in their primitive way they communicated this story to other men, who passed it down to others through the ages, until it became fixed in the memory of the race.

Rachel Carson, *The Sea Around Us*. New York: Oxford University Press, 1951, p. 44.

1968. When this and many of his other absurd prophecies failed to come true, millions of people stopped reading his books.

As Cayce's popularity faded, however, other Atlantologists steadily filled the vacuum he left. Many of them continued a trend that had started in the 1920s, in which they suggested locations for the lost continent other than the Atlantic Ocean. Africa, for instance, became a popular site to place Atlantean civilization. In his 1929 book *Mysterious Sahara*, a Hungarian American named Byron Prorok claimed to have discovered the skeleton of an Atlantean man in the Sahara Desert. Scientists later showed, however, that the remains belonged to a modern North African. Meanwhile, in the same decade, a German geologist, Paul Borchard, insisted that Atlantis had been in what is now Tunisia; and another German, explorer Leo Frobenius, proposed that the lost civilization had been in Nigeria, on Africa's western coast.

Atlantis in Europe, Asia, and Beyond

Later, in the 1950s, theories placing Atlantis in northern Europe gained notoriety. One such proposition came from a respected scholar—marine scientist Rachel Carson, who felt that the Atlantis legend might be based on a society centered in the North Sea (lying along the coasts of Britain and Scandinavia). Another twist on the North Sea theory came in the 1979 book *Atlantis of the North* by German clergyman Jurgen Spanuth. Other European countries suggested to be the original location of Atlantis included Portugal, France, the Netherlands, and the island nation of Malta (in the central Mediterranean Sea).

Did You Know?
Core samples taken from the bottom of the Atlantic Ocean show that the land there has not lain above the ocean's surface for millions of years, if ever.

Still other writers published books or articles that placed Plato's famous lost empire in various parts of Asia. Both Arabia and Iran emerged as possible candidates, as did Sri Lanka, Mongolia, and Crimea (the peninsula jutting into the Black Sea's northern sector). Much farther afield, claims that Brazil and Australia were remnants of the lost Atlantis had their own avid proponents. Some writers even suggested that Antarctica, the frozen continent containing the South Pole, was the site of the Atlantean civilization.

Although the bulk of these hypotheses clearly strained credibility, they were not the most outlandish proposals of the Atlantis literary genre. In the 1984 book *Atlantis: The Eighth Continent*, for example, American language teacher Charles Berlitz claimed that Atlantis had occupied the stretch of ocean popularly known as the Bermuda Triangle. Never offering any solid proof, Berlitz went on to suggest that mysterious domes of hydrogen gas that still plague that region had long ago destroyed Atlantis.

Even more incredible than Berlitz's scenario was one put forward by Atlantologist Shirley Andrews in her 2001 book *Atlantis: Insights from a Lost Civilization*. Extraterrestrials—beings from another world—built Atlantis on Earth, she contended. Presenting not a shred of verifiable evidence, she proposed that the first Atlanteans were "visitors from the heavens whose advice enabled primitive peoples to improve their way of life relatively quickly. Amazing stone constructions attest to the worldwide influence of unknown engineers and builders with sophisticated techniques and skills."[10]

The speculations of Donnelly, Spence, Cayce, Berlitz, and other writers too numerous to name constituted a veritable flood of eager attempts to uncover the true identity of Atlantis. These individuals scoured all the globe's continents and seas and even, in desperation, looked beyond Earth. The vast majority of those writers appeared unaware of a fundamental error they all made and continued to compound. Their mistake was to drift further and further away from their original source material—Plato's texts describing Atlantis and the land he himself inhabited, Greece. In the fullness of time, the Atlantis legend *was* shown to be based in reality. But the lost continent had not existed in some distant, remote location. Instead, as James Mavor puts it, it lay "in a more familiar dimension, in a sea utterly familiar to Plato."[11]

CHAPTER TWO

The Minoan Connection Revealed

During the first half of the twentieth century, and indeed well into the 1960s, the location of Atlantis remained largely a mystery. Popular writers continued to place the lost continent in diverse locales around the globe. Meanwhile, classical historians and scientists were not even convinced Atlantis had been real. The vast majority of them assumed that it had been a figment of Plato's imagination, probably a literary device intended to strengthen a political or moral argument.

One exception among those experts was Greek archaeologist Spyridon Marinatos. He began as a museum director, then served as a professor of ancient history at the University of Athens, and went on to become one of the twentieth century's most distinguished excavators. Over time, he came to suspect that the Atlantis legend was *not* a literary device but rather had been based on fact. Moreover, he contended, the lost civilization Plato had described had been centered somewhere in or near Greece.

Clues from the House of the Lilies

The first link in the long chain of evidence that eventually led Marinatos to that stunning hypothesis was a strange discovery he made in 1932. Then thirty-one years old, he was fascinated by a splendid ancient civilization that had begun to emerge from complete obscurity only a little more than three decades before. In 1900 an older colleague, the great British archaeologist Sir Arthur Evans, started to unearth a huge palace-like structure at Knossos, situated a few kilometers from Crete's northern coast. The building had originally contained hundreds of rooms and corridors on multiple levels and had lain at the hub of a good-sized city. In the years that followed, similar palaces were found elsewhere in Crete. Evans dubbed the powerful Bronze Age maritime people who had built them the Minoans, after the mythical Cretan king Minos.

Did You Know?
In 1939 Marinatos suggested that the disaster that destroyed Atlantis was actually the great Theran eruption.

Just prior to 1930, Marinatos launched his own excavations of Minoan sites in Crete and elsewhere. One of those expeditions took him to Amnisos, a small town on Crete's northern coast that had once served as Knossos's port. There, he found two Minoan villas. One became known as the House of the Lilies after the diggers uncovered a still mostly intact wall painting featuring those flowers.

Although Marinatos was excited about unearthing this well-preserved Minoan structure, he was particularly captivated by the odd manner in which it had been destroyed. As described by his colleague James Mavor,

> During the destruction the walls and corners of the villa had fallen in an unusual way that could not be attributed to an earthquake. The massive stone blocks of the west wall were pushed *outward*, and some of those of the south wall parallel to the sea were missing. He concluded that this could have resulted only from great waves crashing upon the building and then carrying the blocks away in their powerful backwash.[12]

Marinatos realized that a wave that could move such massive stones as if they were toy blocks could be none other than a

The palace of Knossos, built in the Bronze Age by the Minoans, was discovered by British archaeologist Sir Arthur Evans.

tsunami. It also struck him that such a disaster might explain how Minoan civilization collapsed fairly suddenly during the last years of Greece's Bronze Age. The more immediate question, however, was where the giant waves had originated.

It did not take Marinatos long to figure out which kind of disaster had caused the waves and the epicenter of the catastrophe. As he and his assistants continued to excavate the buried buildings at Amnisos, they found layers of volcanic pumice (a lightweight kind of dried lava) covering the entire area. They immediately recognized it as the type of pumice emitted by the volcano on the island of Thera, lying not far north of Crete. Furthermore, the Theran volcano was known to have erupted violently around 1500 BCE, during Greece's late Bronze Age, when Minoan civilization was at its height.

Plato and his fellow classical Greeks did not know of the existence of the Minoan civilization, which predated classical Greece by many centuries. Yet, as Marinatos and other modern scholars came to suspect, the classical Greeks did possess memories of the Minoan world, in garbled form, in some of their beloved myths. One of those stories took the form of the legend of Atlantis, which Plato described in detail in two of his dialogues. Over time, however, historians concluded that echoes of Minoan times exist in other familiar Greek myths.

One is the tale of the Athenian hero Theseus's expedition to Crete, in which he broke into the mazelike Labyrinth and slew a monster—the Minotaur. It now appears certain that this myth reflects the Mycenaean invasion of Minoan Crete. The mazelike structure Theseus captured was undoubtedly the equally mazelike palace-center in the Minoan capital of Knossos.

Another mangled memory of Minoan civilization—one almost perfectly parallel to Plato's Atlantis tale—is the myth of the fabulous island of Scheria. The island was one of the places the Greek hero Odysseus visited during his wanderings following the Trojan War (in Homer's *Odyssey*). Scheria had thirteen kings, one of whom held authority over the others, similar to Atlantis's ten kings, one wielding overall power. In addition, Scheria, Atlantis, and Minoan Crete all had a fertile central plain, complex harbors and docks, and splendid temples dedicated to Poseidon.

After more excavations in the region, in 1939 Marinatos published an article titled "The Volcanic Destruction of Minoan Crete" in the archaeological journal *Antiquity*. Summing up his thesis, he wrote, "I think there is little reason to doubt that the devastation of the coastal sites of Minoan Crete was caused by the waves from the [Bronze Age] eruption of Thera. We read of similar phenomena on the occasion of later eruptions of the same volcano, which in every case were less violent than the one in 1500 B.C."[13]

The Atlantean Connection

At first, Marinatos focused primarily on the great Theran eruption and how it might have brought down the splendid Minoan civilization. Over time, evidence gathered by him and several other scholars showed that the Minoans had indeed been badly crippled by the disaster. Yet they had managed to survive it. They were slowly attempting to rebuild, the evidence indicated, when a second calamity struck. This time it was an invasion by the Greek-speaking Mycenaeans, whose small Bronze Age kingdoms—Athens among them—dotted the nearby Greek mainland.

While studying the possible Athenian implication in the Minoans' downfall, Marinatos noted that some well-known Greek myths described just such an Athenian invasion of Crete. It seemed likely to him that these tales were mangled memories of the real Mycenaean invasion. In turn, this led him to examine another Greek myth that dealt with an invasion by the Bronze Age Athenians. He noticed that in Plato's description of Atlantis, shortly before the Atlanteans' realm was destroyed in a terrible disaster, they had been invaded and defeated by the Athenians. Marinatos now wondered whether the Atlanteans and Minoans were one and the same people.

Did You Know?
In his dialogues, Plato describes Atlantis's size, saying it was 3,000 stadia, which would be about 340 miles (547 km) long.

No sooner had the young excavator speculated on this Atlantean connection to Minoan Crete than it struck him that he had encountered that idea before. After giving it some thought, he remembered that as a teenager he had read a little-known article penned back in 1909. It had made no stir among historians at the time and subsequently had been largely forgotten.

The article's author, a researcher at Queen's University in Belfast, Ireland, named K.T. Frost, had casually pointed out some close parallels between the newly discovered Minoans and Plato's Atlanteans. "Knossos and its allied cities were swept away just when they seemed strongest and safest," Frost wrote. "It was as if the whole kingdom had sunk into the sea, as if the tale of Atlantis were true." He added that Plato's description of Atlantis seemed to him to be "an echo of the Minoans." Moreover, "the whole description of Atlantis which is given in the *Timaeus* and the *Critias* has features so thoroughly Minoan that even Plato could not have invented so many unsuspected facts."[14]

Two Ancient Empires Compared

Marinatos eagerly searched through old newspapers in Greece's national library in Athens, found Frost's article, and reexamined it. Then he refamiliarized himself with Plato's dialogues—the *Timaeus* and the *Critias*—which he had not read in several years. Frost, Marinatos noted, began with Plato's explanation of where the story of Atlantis originated. Plato and his second cousin Critias, the *Timaeus* recounts, were descendants of the great sixth-century BCE Athenian statesman Solon, one of the chief early architects of Athens's famous democracy.

During a long trip to Egypt, Solon had spent time with some local priests, who told him about the fabulous empire of Atlantis. The Atlanteans had fought a major war with Solon's own ancestors, the Athenians, the priests claimed. Not long afterward, Atlantis had been destroyed by a catastrophe. Solon then returned to Greece, Frost said, paraphrasing the *Timaeus*, and told the tale of Atlantis to a relative named Dropides; later, Dropides passed it on to his son; and in this manner it traveled down the generations to Critias and Plato.

Did You Know?

Plato said the Atlantean palace had bathrooms with running water. Bathrooms exactly like that were discovered in the Minoan palace at Knossos.

Next, Marinatos noted, Frost had pointed out a number of startling parallels between the Atlantean empire described by Plato and the Minoan civilization excavated by Evans and other modern archaeologists. First, the Egyptian priests had told Solon that Atlantis had been a large island that had exerted political control over other islands, along with parts of a nearby continent. That had been precisely the political situation with the Minoans, Frost wrote. Evans and other excavators had shown that the Minoans had ruled the large island of Crete and had dominated sections of mainland Greece, itself part of the European continent.

Continuing to pique Marinatos's interest, Frost's article listed other striking parallels between Minoan Crete and Plato's Atlantis.

In his dialogue the *Critias*, Plato went into considerable detail about the complex way the Atlanteans had built their harbors, docks, and the magnificent palace that dominated the island's principal city:

> First of all, they bridged over the [circular] zones of sea [created earlier by Poseidon], which surrounded the ancient metropolis [city], making a road to and from the royal palace. And at the very beginning they built the palace in the habitation of the god and of their ancestors, which they continued to ornament in successive generations, every king surpassing the one who went before him to the utmost of his power, until they made the building a marvel to behold for size and for beauty. And beginning from the sea they bored a canal of three hundred feet [91 m] in width and one hundred feet [30 m] in depth and fifty stadia [6 miles (10 km)] in length, which they carried through to the outermost zone, making a passage from the sea up to this, which became a harbor, and leaving an opening sufficient to enable the largest vessels to find ingress [entrance]. Moreover, they divided at the bridges the zones of land which parted the zones of sea, leaving room for a single trireme [ship with three banks of oars] to pass out of one zone into another, and they covered over the channels so as to leave a way underneath for the ships; for the banks were raised considerably above the water.

Plato, *Critias*, in *The Dialogues of Plato*, trans. Benjamin Jowett. Chicago: Encyclopedia Britannica, 1952, p. 482.

Both places featured large, fertile central plains, for example. Atlantis's plain, Plato wrote, was "surrounded by mountains which descended towards the sea; it was smooth and even, and of an oblong shape [longer than it was wide], [and] sheltered from the north [winds]."[15] In comparison, Frost stated, Crete's central plain of Mesara is also oblong, and it is sheltered from the north winds by a range of mountains.

Another parallel involved Atlantis's singular climate. In the *Critias*, Plato said that the lost continent experienced only two overall seasons—a warm, dry summer and a cool, rainy winter. As Frost pointed out, that was a perfect description of the Mediterranean climate that prevails in southern Greece and the Aegean islands, including Crete. Marinatos, like Frost before him, felt this argued for placing Atlantis in the Mediterranean Sea rather than the Atlantic Ocean.

A City Sleeping and Waiting

Still another similarity between the Minoan and Atlantean realms, Frost stated, was how much the temple of Poseidon in Atlantis's main city resembled the palace-center Evans had uncovered at Knossos. Plato described Poseidon's temple as a massive complex that "they continued to ornament in successive generations, every king surpassing the one who went before him to the utmost of his power, until they made the building a marvel to behold for size and for beauty." Furthermore, Plato said, the temple was some 600 feet (183 m) long and had "a strange barbaric appearance."[16]

Frost went on to say that the Minoan palace-center at Knossos measures about 600 feet on a side, exactly matching the dimensions of the Atlantean temple. As for the "strange barbaric appearance" that Plato had mentioned, both Frost and Marinatos were well aware that Minoan architecture was quite different stylistically in comparison to the classical Greek architecture with which Plato was familiar. As one modern researcher puts it, the Knossos palace-center

> would have looked strange and barbaric to foreigners, and also to those who saw its ruins in later times. The building lacked symmetry, [partly because its] doors were positioned near the corners of rooms as if to provoke curiosity. [Meanwhile] corridors and stairs twisted and turned, roof lines rose and fell, [so that the palace] was built on totally different lines from the temples of [Greece's] classical period.[17]

In examining these and Frost's other close parallels between the Atlantean and Minoan realms, Marinatos noticed one significant discrepancy. Namely, Plato had said that Atlantis's empire had consisted of a large island surrounded by smaller islands. To make the

British researcher K.T. Frost noted that the temple of the Greek god Poseidon (pictured) in Atlantis resembled the palace discovered at Knossos.

parallel complete, therefore, Minoan towns should have existed on several of the islands lying near Crete. However, at the time that Marinatos was reacquainting himself with Frost's Atlantean theory, no Minoan ruins had yet been found on those islands.

What scholars, including Marinatos, did not then realize was that a major Minoan city *did* exist on one of those islands—none other than Thera. The problem was that it lay buried beneath layers of volcanic debris. Over the course of many centuries, a series of civilizations had risen and fallen around it. All the while, its secrets, which were destined to eventually help solve the mystery of Atlantis, had remained locked away from an unsuspecting world. In scholar Charles Pellegrino's words, even as most of Egypt's splendid pyramids "crumbled into mere ghost images of their former glory, a city slept unperceived within the earth, astonishingly intact, waiting only for the twentieth century and Spyridon Marinatos."[18]

CHAPTER THREE

Memories of Minoan Glories

The more that Spyridon Marinatos studied the parallels between the legend of Atlantis and the very real Minoan civilization, the more he realized that these could not be mere coincidences of history. Some of the details of the ancient Minoan culture that he and other archaeologists continued to uncover were exact matches for details of the Atlantean culture Plato had described. This convinced an increasing number of classical scholars that the story of Atlantis was a surviving memory of the glories of the lost Minoan civilization.

For decades, Marinatos remained at the center of speculation about Atlantis's true identity in part because he stood at the forefront of excavations and studies of the ancient Minoans. Moreover, he confirmed that position in the late 1960s when he stunned the world with his discovery of an entire, largely intact Bronze Age Minoan town. Called Akrotiri, it is located on the southern rim of Santorini/Thera. The artifacts Marinatos and later excavators found there, including wall paintings still retaining their original colors, hugely amplified knowledge of ancient Minoan culture. In turn, this allowed scholars to match various details of Minoan culture with corresponding details in Plato's account of Atlantean culture.

Identical Economies

Even before the discovery of Akrotiri, Marinatos and his colleagues had already established a number of such supportive details. For example, it was known that both the Atlanteans and Minoans had large, mazelike structures dedicated to the god Poseidon in their capital cities; also, both had engaged in a war with the Bronze Age Athenians; and both had been devastated by a large-scale disaster. To these, over time, Marinatos and other scholars were able to add even more comparisons, some of them amazingly detailed.

First, Plato had described the Atlantean economy as resting partly on a vast foreign trade. Because of the great size and reputation of Atlantis's empire, Plato said, "many things were brought to them from foreign countries."[19] Similarly, excavations at Knossos in Crete and Akrotiri in Thera showed that the Minoans had large merchant fleets that traded with lands far and wide.

The other major portion of the Atlantean economy was based on domestic agriculture and livestock raising, Plato reported. "There was an abundance of wood for carpenter's work and sufficient maintenance for tame and wild animals." Furthermore, "whatever fragrant things there now are in the earth, whether roots or herbage, or woods, or essences which distil from fruit and flower, grew and thrived in that land" and all "in infinite abaundance."[20] The discoveries made at Akrotiri, along with what was already known from studying the Minoan palace-centers on Crete, showed that in identical fashion the Minoan economy was supported by farming and animal husbandry. The bulk of the local inhabitants in the Minoan island communities were farmers who grew crops and/or raised animals, including sheep, goats, pigs, and cattle.

Typically, Minoan farmers lived in small villages located within walking distance of their fields. Although Akrotiri was a good-sized town, like the one that once surrounded the Knossos palace-center, evidence suggests that Thera featured numerous small farming villages that supported the main town. A typical farmhouse in such a village featured a central living space about the size of a small

Did You Know?
Plato called Atlantis's first king Eumelos, and scholars point out that Melos is an Aegean island that was once part of the Minoan empire.

Tourists explore the ruins of the Bronze Age Minoan city of Akrotiri. The city was discovered in the 1960s largely intact and allowed scholars to match details of Minoan culture with descriptions of Atlantean culture.

bedroom in a modern American home. The floor was made of hard-beaten earth, and a wooden pillar supported the ceiling. Four to six smaller rooms—some storerooms, others bedrooms—flanked the sides of the central room.

The Advanced Plumbing Parallel

The Minoan farmhouses did not have formal bathrooms. Like the vast majority of farmers across the world before the twentieth century, Minoan farmers of average means relieved themselves in outhouses. However, better-off Minoan city dwellers *did* have bathrooms, often equipped with modern-style plumbing, including toilets with drains for carrying away waste. The waste from a toilet in Akrotiri went through a pipe into a town sewer system. The luxurious apartments in the Minoan palace-centers were also equipped with modern-style bathrooms.

They featured running water, often captured in rain catchers called cisterns and carried into a bathroom through pipes made of baked clay. In addition, some of the water was heated in kiln-like furnaces fueled by burning wood.

To many archaeologists, including Marinatos, the advanced bathroom facilities they had found in Minoan structures matched the Atlantean plumbing facilities Plato had described too closely to be mere coincidence. A passage in the *Critias* says that the Atlanteans "made cisterns, some open to the heavens, others roofed over to be used in winter as warm baths. There were the king's baths, and the baths of private persons, [and] there were separate baths for women."[21]

Faced with this incredibly close parallel involving sophisticated plumbing facilities, archaeologists immediately noted that nowhere in the world had such advances ever been found in a Bronze Age society. Not until some fifteen centuries later did Roman engineers begin to build facilities comparable to them, which made the Minoan examples completely unique in their time. This means that the folk memory of advanced bathrooms that Plato preserved in his *Critias* could not have been based on any culture other than the Minoan one. As J.V. Luce phrased it, these details "seem to provide quite strong circumstantial evidence for identifying Atlantis with Crete."[22]

Did You Know?
Some Minoan bathrooms featured the oldest-known flush toilets, in which rainwater held in cisterns carried away the wastes.

The Very Same Bull Rituals

As archaeologists continued to excavate at Akrotiri, Knossos, and other ancient Minoan sites, they uncovered other strong cultural parallels between the Atlantean and Minoan civilizations. One of the more striking examples involved a specific religious feature shared by the Atlantean temple that Plato described and the Minoan palace-centers on Crete. This feature consisted of a bull

Bull Leaping: A Serious Religious Ritual

Religious rituals surrounding bulls were central to Atlantean religion, as Plato emphasized in the *Critias*. Indeed, he said that bulls actually roamed through the great temple of Poseidon in Atlantis's capital. Greek archaeologist Spyridon Marinatos was among the earliest of many modern experts to point out that only one known ancient culture in the entire world actually featured bull worship that included bringing living bulls inside a palace or temple. It was the Minoan culture, in which worshippers watched young, acrobatic men and women leaping over the backs of huge, snorting bulls. According to researcher Rodney Castleden in his complex study of Minoan civilization, this bull leaping was "a ceremony that was itself central to the Minoan belief system." He adds,

> Parallels between Minoan bull-leaping and Spanish bull-fighting should not deceive us into seeing bull-leaping as mere "theater of cruelty" entertainment. It was not a game, but a serious and central ritual in the Minoan belief system. The bull was a manifestation of Poteidan [the early form of Poseidon worshipped by the Minoans], and dancing with the most powerful god in the Minoan pantheon was no light matter. Probably the bull dance expressed the interweaving of human and divine destinies. There were elements of collusion [getting along] and elements of struggle with the deity. Probably the ritual was an ordeal, one of many rites of passage that young Minoans, girls as well as boys, had to undergo in order to achieve higher status.

Rodney Castleden, *Minoans: Life in Bronze Age Crete.* New York: Routledge, 2002, pp. 146, 148.

cult—a set of rituals and visual imagery supporting a deeply felt reverence for bulls.

This parallel begins with what Plato said about the cult. "There were bulls who had the range of the temple of Poseidon,"[23] he said. It has already been established that the Poseidon temple in Atlantis and the palace-center at Knossos are likely the same structure. For the bull parallel to have weight, it would need to be shown that bulls and bull worship were a major preoccupation of the Minoans who lived in and ran the Knossos palace. Sure enough, surviving wall paintings, carved statues and figurines, and other evidence clearly indicate that the locals regularly brought bulls inside the palace for use in elaborate rituals. These included games, watched by throngs of eager spectators, in which young men and women leaped over the bulls' backs.

Did You Know?
The famous Minoan bull-leaping fresco was discovered by British archaeologist Sir Arthur Evans in 1917 in the palace-center at Knossos.

Even more stunning is a specific and minute detail of the bull cult that both the Atlanteans and Minoans shared. Regarding the hunting ritual that captured the creatures in the first place, Plato said the Atlanteans "hunted the bulls without weapons but with staves [wooden sticks] and nooses." Later, after the bull games were over and the creatures were sacrificed, religious officials "filled a bowl of wine and cast in a clot of [bull's] blood for each of them" and then "drew [wine] from the bowl in golden cups."[24]

Early in the twentieth century two Minoan golden goblets, which came to be called the Vapheio cups, were found. Carved on their sides is a highly detailed scene in which men hunt bulls using

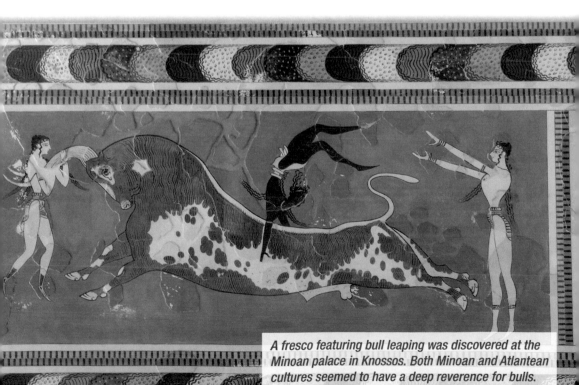

A fresco featuring bull leaping was discovered at the Minoan palace in Knossos. Both Minoan and Atlantean cultures seemed to have a deep reverence for bulls.

sticks and nooses. Frost pointed out that "Plato's words exactly describe the scenes on the famous Vapheio cups, which certainly represent catching wild bulls for the Minoan [bull ritual], which, as we know from the palace itself, differed from all others which the world has seen."[25] Moreover, some historians have asserted that the Vapheio cups are likely among the actual "golden cups" used by the religious officials in the *Critias*. No mention is made in Plato's dialogue of what those Atlantean priests looked like or how they dressed when carrying out the sacred rituals. But some modern scholars think that a glimpse of them may have been preserved in a separate Greek myth. In the famous story of Theseus's voyage to Crete, he entered the Labyrinth and killed the Minotaur. That beast was said to have the body of a man and the head of a bull. It is possible, some experts say, that Minoan and Atlantean priests wore bull masks during their rituals, a singular image that was later distorted into the legend of the fearsome Minotaur.

Military Parallels

Often overshadowed by the widely popular bull rituals in studies of Minoan civilization is the question of Minoan weaponry. Because the Minoans had large fleets of ships that guarded their islands, it is frequently assumed that they did not require land armies. This idea is false, however, for abundant evidence of Minoan battle helmets, swords, spears, and armor was found during the twentieth century. This fact matches Plato's description of Atlantean soldiers, including archers, horsemen, slingers (armed with stone-hurling slings), javelin throwers, and others.

Another aspect of weapons and warfare in which there is a strong parallel between Atlantis and Minoan Crete is the use of chariots. Plato said that each Atlantean leader was required to furnish war chariots for the country's army; moreover, he told how each chariot had to be accompanied by "a pair of chariot-horses."[26] This established that Atlantean chariots were drawn by two horses, not one, three, or four, which some other ancient peoples employed at one time or another.

In his dialogue the *Critias*, Plato described Atlantean soldiers and weapons. Modern scholars point out that these descriptions sound very much like those employed by the ancient Egyptians, ancient Greeks, and other ancient eastern Mediterranean peoples. It may be that he interpreted this similarity to suggest that peoples everywhere shared the same military traditions and practices. If so, he was incorrect. Apparently it did not occur to Plato that this resemblance might be due to the fact that Atlantis itself had been situated in the eastern Mediterranean region. In the *Critias*, he stated that

> the leader [of each section of Atlantis] was required to furnish for the war the sixth portion of a war-chariot, so as to make up a total of ten thousand chariots. Also, two horses and riders for them, and a pair of chariot-horses without a seat, accompanied by a horseman who could fight on foot carrying a small shield, and having a charioteer who stood behind the man-at-arms to guide the two horses. Also, he was bound to furnish two heavy-armed soldiers, two slingers, three stone-shooters, and three javelin-men, who were light-armed, and four sailors to make up the complement of twelve hundred ships.

Plato, *Critias*, in *The Dialogues of Plato*, trans. Benjamin Jowett. Chicago: Encyclopedia Britannica, 1952, p. 484.

Similarly, as researcher Rodney Castleden points out, "the Minoans used chariots in battle," which were shaped the same as Mycenaean versions from mainland Greece. After describing a Minoan chariot in fair detail, he makes the important point that "a wooden bar or frame extended forwards between the two ponies who drew the chariot along."[27] Therefore, both Atlantean and Minoan chariots were drawn by two horses.

The Other Pillars

Plato likely took the time and effort to describe Atlantean soldiers and weapons because he felt the need to explain how Atlantis had managed to conquer many other nations and thereby forge a mighty empire. To muster an army and navy large enough to accomplish military operations of that magnitude clearly required a massive population base from which to draw the necessary manpower. In turn, to support such a large population, Plato reasoned, Atlantis must have been a very big island.

In fact, the estimate given to Plato's ancestor Solon by the Egyptian priests was that Atlantis was "an island greater in extent than Libya and Asia" combined. A landmass that big obviously could not have fit into the Mediterranean basin; hence, the priests reasoned, it must have been located "outside the Pillars of Heracles,"[28] in the much larger Atlantic Ocean. Plato clearly accepted this location for the lost continent.

The Pillars of Heracles (or Hercules, as the Romans called that mythical hero) was the ancient name for the two stony outcrops that line the gap through which the Mediterranean Sea opens into the Atlantic. One of them is the famous Rock of Gibraltar. The key question, from the viewpoint of modern historians, is whether these were the pillars to which the Egyptian priests referred.

The fact is that before about 600 BCE the peoples of the ancient eastern Mediterranean region called at least two different geographic sites the Pillars of Heracles. In addition to the one bordering the Atlantic, the other consisted of the two southernmost peninsulas of mainland Greece—Cape Tainaron and Cape Malea. These peninsulas point directly at Crete, located only a few miles to the east. They were almost certainly the pillars the Egyptian priests mentioned to Solon, Castleden contends. The "large island with one end just outside the Pillars of Heracles could only have meant Crete,"[29] he writes.

Furthermore, Marinatos's colleague, Greek seismologist Angelos Galanopoulos, pointed out a frequently overlooked passage in Plato's *Timaeus*. It says that the Egyptian priests told Solon that the Atlanteans ruled over the area stretching "as far as Egypt" in one direction and "as far as Tyrrhenia [Italy]"[30] in the other direction. That appears to place Atlantis about half way between Egypt and Italy—in the region of Greece, not the faraway Atlantic Ocean. To the growing community of historians and scientists whom Marinatos had inspired, evidence of this sort, linking the Atlantean and Minoan civilizations, continued to mount.

CHAPTER FOUR

A Blast That Shook the World

Having established that the island Plato called Atlantis lay in the eastern Mediterranean Sea rather than the Atlantic Ocean, Marinatos and other scholars addressed one hugely crucial detail of the Atlantis story. It was the enormous natural disaster that Plato said had destroyed that mysterious continent. Here, the experts already strongly suspected that the evidence of large tsunamis, which Marinatos had uncovered in northern Crete in the 1930s, might well be related to the story of Atlantis's demise.

Marinatos had long been convinced that those giant, destructive waves had been generated by an eruption of the volcano that is today located in Thera's central bay. Like modern geologists, volcanologists, and other scientists, he knew that that mountain had exploded violently during the Bronze Age. Indeed, by the late 1800s firm evidence showed that sometime between 1650 and 1450 BCE the Theran volcano had produced the largest natural disaster on the planet since human record keeping had begun several thousand years ago. During the last four decades of the twentieth century, Marinatos and other experts showed that Thera's blast had not only shaken the world in the figurative sense but had also been forever memorialized as the culprit in the legend of Atlantis's catastrophic end.

This illustration depicts the destruction of Atlantis. Scholars are convinced that the waves that destroyed it were generated by a large volcanic eruption nearby.

A Monster Lurking Below

When the *Chain*, the ship carrying the members of the 1966 Woods Hole–sponsored expedition, entered Thera's central bay, the team's leader, James Mavor, was awestruck. Even after the passage of three and a half millennia, he later recalled, the evidence of the Bronze Age eruption was still stark and overpowering. The great seismologist Angelos Galanopoulos "was the only one on board who had seen the island previously," Mavor wrote, "and his anticipation matched my own. The impressive volcanic remnant materialized full force and provided a striking sight as we headed into the caldera."[31]

Ever since the great eruption, Thera's caldera, or volcanic crater, has been filled with water, forming the central bay. That roughly oval-shaped waterway, Mavor said, "is about 9 miles [14 km] in the north-south direction and about 7 miles [11 km] in the east-west. All around us, the black cliffs, so steep that the ancient lava flows and pumice falls were clearly outlined, formed the sides of this great bowl. The water, 1,300 feet [396 m] to the bottom, was deeper than the cliffs were high."[32]

Meanwhile, in the bay's center lay the tiny island of Nea Kaimeni, which formed during a more recent outburst of the still-active monster volcano lurking below. Like scientists who had studied Thera's geography before them, Mavor, Galanopoulos, and their team realized that the huge bay and towering cliffs surrounding Nea Kaimeni are remnants of the shattering Bronze Age eruption. They knew that before that disaster, the bay through which the *Chain* now moved did not yet exist. Instead, during the early Bronze Age, Thera had been a single, roughly round island some 11 miles (18 km) in diameter. Indeed, its original name was not Thera but, appropriately, Strongyle, meaning "the round one." Back in that ancient era, a massive volcanic cone loomed in Strongyle's central region. (Some volcanologists think there might have been two separate cones standing side by side.)

Did You Know?
The towering vertical cliffs lining Thera's bay today are the upper sections of the walls of the caldera formed by the volcano's catastrophic collapse.

The Climactic Collapse

Using the sophisticated electronic instruments aboard the *Chain*, Mavor and Galanopoulos carefully studied the ocean floor beneath Thera's bay as well as the cliffs and other massive geological features that surrounded them. Their studies confirmed, refined, and to some degree expanded existing knowledge of the great eruption. In the early stages of that cataclysm, they learned, the volcanic cone (or cones) expelled immense quantities of ash, pumice, and other debris. Geological evidence suggests that these initial outpourings happened in stages, each preceded by earthquakes and each more violent than the last. Archaeological evidence subsequently confirmed this. Marinatos's excavations at Akrotiri a few years later showed that the town's residents had had time to evacuate before the final and worst volcanic blast.

That explosion was so enormous that anyone still on the island would have been instantly deafened seconds before being torn limb from limb by the force of the blast. The earlier discharges had partially emptied the huge chamber filled with magma. For many centuries that magma, compacted by gigantic pressures from deep underground, had pushed outward, in the process supporting and maintaining the mountain's heavy outer layers. But when the chamber emptied completely during the eruption's last phase, gravity's mighty hand abruptly took over. The island's entire central section, now unsupported, suddenly collapsed inward, creating an enormous caldera.

Did You Know?

The waves generated by the collapse of the Krakatoan volcano obliterated more than 290 Indonesian towns and villages.

Immediately after this vast void formed, untold millions of gallons of seawater flooded into it. The energy expended by this moving liquid was so great that as the water reached the crater's center, it rebounded with colossal force, generating towering tsunamis that expanded outward in all directions. Minutes later, some of those waves crashed ashore at Amnisos on Crete's northern coast and demolished the villas that eons later Spyridon Marinatos would excavate and study.

The Krakatoan Parallel

It was not simply the evidence gathered by instruments like those aboard the *Chain* that allowed Marinatos, Galanopoulos, Mavor, and others to piece together Thera's ancient collapse scenario. Fortunately for modern experts, the existence of other volcanic

Some key clues linking Thera's massive Bronze Age eruption to the ruin of the Minoan/Atlantean civilization were discoveries of the devastation wrought by giant sea waves and pumice in northern Crete. Directly facing the eruption's oncoming blast and wave effects, that area received the full brunt of Thera's wrath. Noted English researcher Rodney Castleden summarizes the overwhelming evidence:

> The seashore villa excavated by Marinatos [in 1932] had several huge blocks in its foundation course shoved sideways. They can still be seen today. And the only way they could have been displaced is by pushing or dragging by a very large volume of water. Since the Minoan coastline was probably 50 meters [164 ft] away, only a tsunami could have had this impact on the house. Pumice deposited among the foundations adds corroborative evidence that it was tsunamis at the time of the Thera eruption that were to blame. Theran pumice has been found 10 to 15 meters [33 to 49 ft] above sea level behind the villa. A shrine in the small temple [nearby] contained tiny offering cups. The Minoans had put pieces of pumice in them, presumably as [religious] offerings back to Poseidon. Here we glimpse the primitive terror inspired by the arrival of the Theran pumice. Why would it have inspired this response unless it had arrived with a tsunami [since Poseidon was thought to cause tsunamis]?

Rodney Castleden, *Atlantis Destroyed*. New York: Routledge, 2001, p. 125.

calderas around the world provided extra models to study. In particular, the world had witnessed a large-scale caldera form in real time in 1883. The event took place on the small island of Krakatoa, lying in the narrow strait between the much bigger Indonesian islands of Sumatra and Java. Initially, the volcano spewed out ash and pumice in minor outbursts that occurred at intervals. But these stages of the eruption led up to a far larger explosion, after which the mountain's tall cone collapsed, creating a caldera. When the surrounding sea poured into the huge cavity, tsunamis rushed outward and pounded the nearby heavily populated coasts.

Marinatos reasoned that a study of Krakatoa's eruption would produce important insights about Thera's Bronze Age outburst. In his 1939 paper in *Antiquity*, he discussed the Krakatoan disaster: "A tremendous roar accompanied the explosion and was heard over 2,000 miles [3,219 km] away—just one-twelfth of the earth's circumference. [But] worst of all was a series of terrific waves which rose after the explosion. They were as much as 90 feet [27 m] high, and broke with devastating force and speed against the coasts of Java and Sumatra." In some places, Marinatos went on, even after traveling inland for more than 0.5 miles (0.8 km), the waves were still some 45 feet (14 m) high. "Whole towns, villages and woods were destroyed [and] the amazing catastrophe cost over 36,000 lives."[33]

Marinatos also pointed out that although the Krakatoan event was devastating, Thera's eruption was likely much *more* destructive. In part, he wrote, this was because the island of Krakatoa is

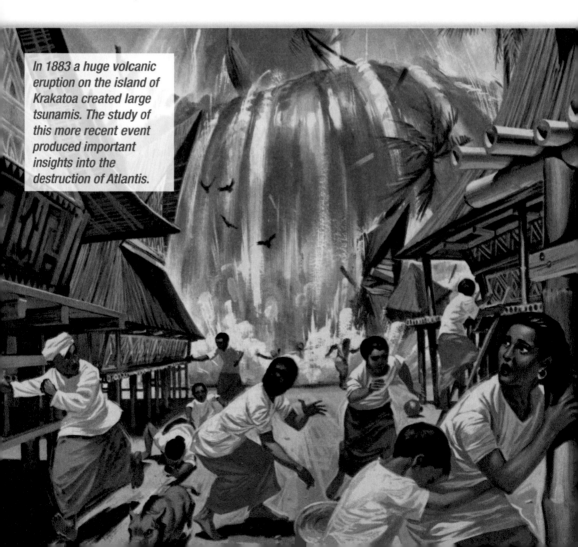

In 1883 a huge volcanic eruption on the island of Krakatoa created large tsunamis. The study of this more recent event produced important insights into the destruction of Atlantis.

considerably smaller than Thera. He estimated that about 9 square miles (23 sq km) of Krakatoa's landmass collapsed, compared to 32 square miles (83 sq km) in Thera's case. Other experts later corroborated Marinatos's estimate that the Theran collapse generated roughly four times as much energy as the Krakatoan one.

What is more, the water lying between Thera and northern Crete is several times deeper than that between Java and Sumatra; and the deeper the water, the larger the waves that will be produced by a given amount of energy. This means that the tsunamis that struck ancient Crete in the minutes following Thera's collapse were much larger than the ones that killed more than thirty-six thousand Indonesians in 1883. Although most of the Minoan palace-centers were situated a bit inland from the coast, the waves would have raced toward them at up to 20 miles per hour (32 km/h) and struck with tremendous force. "The mud-brick upper stories of the tall Cretan palaces and mansions," J.V. Luce remarks, would "have suffered very severely." He estimates that the loss of life was probably "many times as great" in Minoan Crete thirty-five centuries ago as it was in Indonesia in 1883. On top of the tsunami damage, Luce adds,

> the hills and valleys of eastern Crete were covered to a considerable depth of ash fall-out [and] the Minoans of central and eastern Crete who escaped the waves may well have found much of their land uncultivable, their orchards destroyed, [and] their buildings flattened. This factor of fall-out could be the explanation for [the] westward migration [of the Minoan population] which is clear from the archaeological evidence.[34]

How Distant Observers Saw the Disaster

Luce refers to the fact that prior to the eruption, the bulk of Minoan farms had been in the eastern portion of Crete. The ashfall and waves caused the worst damage in that region, prompting many of the survivors to migrate to western Crete. Ultimately, however, Luce and other scholars point out, this move proved futile. In addition to countless lives and their best farms, the Minoans had surely lost most of their ships, the source of at least half their economy. Their entire way of life had been badly crippled. Although they began trying to rebuild, it is not surprising that they were unable to withstand the ensuing, unexpected invasion by the opportunistic Mycenaean warlords.

Considering the large amount of clear-cut geological and historical evidence available, there was only one conclusion that Luce, Marinatos, and other modern scholars could reach. Namely, the dire effects of the Theran catastrophe had at least initiated the demise of Minoan civilization. Moreover, the resemblance of that volcanic disaster scenario to the one Plato described in his dialogues was undeniable. Atlantis had sunk into the sea, he wrote. In similar fashion, most of the island originally called Strongyle, and later renamed Thera, had collapsed into a watery grave.

Marinatos, Luce, and their colleagues did need to address one inconsistency in this broad parallel between the Minoan and Atlantean calamities. Most of Thera had indeed disappeared beneath the waves. Yet the Minoan civilization's main focus and the bulk of its population lay on Crete, and that large island remained very much intact.

In an article titled "On the Atlantis Legend," Marinatos argued that this discrepancy was fairly easy to explain by examining the origin of Plato's information about Atlantis. Some Egyptian priests had told Plato's ancestor Solon the story. Thus, that story was colored by the point of view of observers who lived hundreds of miles to the southeast of the Minoan heartland. The Egyptians *were* familiar with Minoan merchants, with whom they sometimes traded. Yet most of Egypt's residents knew little or nothing about those traders' faraway homeland, including which of its many islands contained the core of Minoan culture. Thus, Marinatos concluded, hearing that a terrible disaster had struck the Minoans, in their mind's eye the Egyptians combined the separate Minoan islands into a single one. "The Egyptians heard about the sinking of an island," Marinatos wrote, "which was Thera. But this island, small and insignificant, was unknown to them. This event they transferred to the neighbor-

It stands to reason that the giant waves generated by the Theran volcano's collapse would be remembered in the folklore of the peoples living at that time in the lands bordering the Aegean Sea. This is indeed the case, as descriptions of those waves abound in Greek mythology. The striking example cited here is from the fifth-century BCE Athenian playwright Euripides's play *Hippolytus*. A messenger enters and tells of a disaster he has just witnessed on a beach on the Saronic Gulf. A large inlet of the Aegean Sea lying not far from Athens, its low-lying shores would have been among the prime targets of the Theran tsunamis. The messenger recalls,

> There is a stretch of shore that lies already facing the Saronic Gulf. Here, from the ground, a roar like Zeus's thunderclap came [and was] terrible to hear. The horses raised their heads and pricked their ears right up [and] on us fell a lively fear, wondering what the sound could be. And when we looked upon the foaming shores, we saw a monstrous wave towering up to the sky, so big it [hid] the isthmus and Asclepius's rock. Next, swelling up and surging onward, [it] neared the shore where stood the four-horse chariot. And in the very surge and breaking of the flood, the wave threw up a bull, a fierce and monstrous thing, and with his bellowing the land was wholly filled [with water]. As for us who saw the sight, it seemed too much for eyes to look upon.

Euripides, *Hippolytus*, in *Three Great Plays by Euripides*, trans. Rex Warner. New York: New American Library, 1958, pp. 117–18.

ing Crete, an island which was dreadfully struck [by a disaster] and with which they had lost contact suddenly."[35]

Surviving Memories in Folklore

As classical scholars continued to piece together the connection between Thera's Bronze Age eruption and the disaster that destroyed Atlantis, they often reexamined the Greek myths. Thera's collapse and its aftereffects had added up to a truly enormous historical event. Surely, Marinatos and his fellow investigators argued, some aspects of a catastrophe of such humongous proportions must have been preserved in the subsequent folklore of the Greek region.

Sure enough, the experts discovered, the Greek myths are filled with such folk memories. Most are couched in religious allegory—that is, morality tales in which angry gods punish individuals or entire peoples for various misdeeds. Yet as Luce and other scholars have pointed out, the connection between these tales and the Theran disaster is plain to see. Geological evidence shows that no other catastrophe of such magnitude struck Greece in the late Bronze Age; hence, by default, those stories that are based on a real disaster must be echoes of the Theran eruption.

One dramatic example is the early Greek epic poet Hesiod's description of a titanic battle between Zeus, the leader of the Greek gods, and the giant monster Typhon. When the religious trappings are removed, what remains is a vivid folk memory of Thera's monstrous blasts, ashfalls, collapse, and the ensuing tsunamis. "The whole earth boiled, and heaven and the sea," Hesiod wrote. "The great waves raged along the shore [and] endless quakes arose." There was a "blazing fire in the mountain hollows, [and] reckless gusts blow on the sea [and] bring calamity to [humans], shattering ships and killing sailors." In addition, these giant waves "over the vast and blooming earth blast the lovely fields of earthborn men and fill the land with dust and dreadful noise."[36]

Folk memories of the disaster abound in other myths as well. Many of them mention the sea god Poseidon, whom Plato said was Atlantis's patron deity, and how he unleashed massive sea waves. In one well-known story, for instance, Poseidon—angry with the Athenians—floods the low-lying plain situated between Athens's urban center and the sea. In another tale, the same god makes the sea rush inland and drown the Argive plain in southeastern Greece. In still another myth, Poseidon causes a huge wave to flood the lands lying near Lycia on the Aegean Sea's eastern coast. Galanopoulos is one of many scholars who feel that these and other early Greek flood legends, most involving the same god who drowned Atlantis, create a powerful link between the Theran and Atlantean disasters. "Only an event as catastrophic as the Thera collapse," he says, "could have this effect."[37]

CHAPTER FIVE

Atlantis's Last Days Revisited

Thanks to the discovery of a great deal of archaeological, literary, geological, and other evidence, by the twenty-first century many classical scholars and scientists had formed a strong, complex theory to explain the famous tale of Atlantis. Namely, they contend, it was inspired by the Bronze Age Minoan civilization and its calamitous demise. Indeed, "the idea that Atlantis might be a memory of the fabulous palaces, courts, and temples of Minoan Crete," historical researcher Andrew Collins writes, "is today the most academically accepted theory on the origins of the Atlantis legend."[38]

University of Melbourne archaeologist Dora Constantinidis, who has closely examined the once-buried Theran town of Akrotiri, agrees. Excavations there and on Crete, she points out, have revealed a lost civilization almost exactly like the one Plato described in his dialogues. "The more you look at the remains at Akrotiri," she remarks, "there are so many elements of the [Atlantis] story that you can see in the wall paintings."[39]

Constantinidis and other experts have used the various kinds of evidence compiled about the Minoans and their untimely fall to piece together a plausible scenario of those momentous Bronze Age events. It is a compelling tale of the emergence of Europe's first advanced culture. At the height of their glory, the evidence suggests, a catastrophe of immense proportions overwhelmed the Minoans. This calamity laid the foundations of the timeless legend of lost Atlantis.

Thera's Formation and Settlement

This remarkable story begins deep in the mists of a past age, when no people yet inhabited Crete, Thera, and the other Aegean islands. Millions of years ago, in the spot Thera now occupies, a volcano suddenly burst upward from the seafloor and began growing. In later eruptions, spanning countless centuries, the new mountain gained height and breadth until its top cleared the sea's surface. As many more millennia passed, bringing still more eruptions unseen by human eyes, the new volcanic island continued to expand. Roughly circular in shape, eventually it measured more than 10 miles (16 km) across; at its center loomed a massive, steep-sided cone that towered thousands of feet into the sky.

Still more time passed. During the calm periods between eruptions, grass, trees, vines, and other plants took root in the rich volcanic soil. As a result, the island became lush and inviting and thereby attracted its first human settlers. They arrived

The coastal city of Akrotiri is depicted in this fresco. The city was important to the Minoans as a central port in the Aegean islands.

in about 4500 BCE, some sixty-five centuries ago, likely having migrated from the nearby Greek mainland.

These early Therans built villages and farmed the relatively flat lands lying along the great cone's lower slopes. Now and then earthquakes rocked the island, causing damage that ranged from minor to heavy. Yet even when the latter occurred, the residents always rebuilt their homes. One of those villages, located on the island's southern rim, steadily grew into the prosperous town of Akrotiri. Sometime between 1950 and 1850 BCE, its inhabitants were drawn into the expanding orbit of the Minoans, centered in nearby Crete. It is not surprising that the Minoans would seek to make Thera an outpost. As Rodney Castleden points out, though small, that island "was in a key position, the link between the [central Aegean islands] and Crete. As such, it was a natural conduit for Cretan influence, a stepping-stone between Crete, Melos, Kea, Paros, Naxos, and mainland Greece."[40]

As time went on, the Therans regularly traded foodstuffs, pottery, and other goods with the Minoans. In addition, as Minoan culture spread outward and "began to swamp the Aegean,"[41] in one historian's words, Thera felt its influences. The Therans learned the Minoan language and adopted Minoan dress and other customs. By around 1700 BCE, Akrotiri was mostly, if not fully, a Minoan town.

Did You Know?
The Minoan palace-centers were not simply royal residences. They also served as storehouses and redistribution depots for food and other domestic goods.

A Vast Maritime Empire

On Crete, meanwhile, the center of Minoan population and power, the palace-centers at Knossos and elsewhere had become sprawling, splendid structures covering many acres and containing bathrooms with running water and heated pools. Moreover, the Minoan heartland now oversaw a vast maritime empire based mostly on shipping and trade. Spanish scholar Mireia Movellán Luis writes,

> As Minoan culture and trade radiated across the Aegean, communities on the islands [near] the coast of modern-day Turkey were radically changed through contact with Crete. Cretan fashions became very popular [and] local island elites first acquired Cretan pottery and textiles as a symbol of prestige. Later, the presence of Minoan merchants also prompted island communities far from Knossos to adopt Crete's standard system of weights and measures, [and] the Minoans also maintained trading relationships with Egypt, Syria, [Italy], and the Greek mainland.[42]

That relationship with mainland Greece would prove especially crucial over time. The mainlanders, whom historians call the Mycenaeans, lived in small kingdoms, among them Mycenae, Athens, Tiryns, and Thebes. For centuries they borrowed most of their dress and artistic styles from the Minoans. Much of the mainlanders' cultural backwardness stemmed from the fact that they were initially landlubbers with few ships and seafaring traditions. For this reason, the Minoans long dominated them economically and likely also politically, which must have caused resentment among the Mycenaeans.

Did You Know?
Evidence suggests that when Thera's volcano collapsed, close to half of the town of Akrotiri disappeared into the caldera.

What neither the Minoans nor Mycenaeans could foresee at the time was that political and other affairs in the region were about to alter radically. Furthermore, the change would be driven by a unique combination of human and natural causes. Regarding the latter, enormous geological forces were already gathering beneath the Aegean seabed. That unstoppable process would lead to the Theran volcano's most spectacular outburst in more than a million years.

48

The Therans Abandon Their Homes

The great Greek archaeologist Spyridon Marinatos raised a daughter, Nanno (born 1950), who also became a noted archaeologist. In her popular book about art and religion in ancient Minoan Thera, she presents a likely scenario for the abandonment of the island by its residents shortly before the great late Bronze Age volcanic eruption. These conclusions are based on detailed evidence found by excavators in the ruins of the Theran town of Akrotiri. Because of damage caused by one of the pre-eruption earthquakes, she writes,

> the town already lay in ruins when the eruption of the volcano occurred and buried it under the ashes. [On] the ruined walls, grass had begun to grow. Thus, at least one rainy season had intervened between the earth-quake and the eruption. It was the earthquake that forced the inhabitants to leave. [The residents] gathered together their valuables and left. No jewelry or precious metals have been recovered from the site. Only a few bronze vessels and daggers were forgotten. The bulk of finds consist of pottery, which is both impractical to carry away and cheap to manufac-ture. A few people remained behind and lived a precarious existence in the ruins. . . . In the 1930s, Spyridon Marinatos formulated a theory that postulated a volcanic destruction of Minoan Crete. [At] the time, very few scholars took his theory seriously. When, however, he excavated Akrotiri in the late 1960s, it was thought that his theory had been vindicated.

Nanno Marinatos, *Art and Religion in Thera: Reconstructing a Bronze Age Society.* Athens: D. and I. Ma-thioulakis, 2001, p. 29.

The first sign of trouble was a series of periodic earthquakes in the southern Aegean islands, centered at Thera, probably begin-ning in the early or mid-1600s BCE. The quakes grew larger over time, and geological evidence shows that one was accompanied by a moderate-sized outpouring of ash from the Theran volcano's cone. Fearing that worse dangers might follow, many of Thera's residents left their homes and sailed to various nearby islands.

There followed a quiet period that may have lasted as long as a few years. Reasoning that it was now safe, many people returned to the island and started repairing those structures damaged by the quakes. Some of these projects were still ongoing when the biggest quake and ashfall yet suddenly struck. This time virtually all the inhabitants fled. (Marinatos and other excavators surmised this from the absence of human skeletons in Akrotiri's ruins.)

Stupendous Energy

Leaving the island proved prudent, for soon the eruption approached its dreadful culmination. Initially, gigantic quantities of finely granulated ash poured skyward from the volcanic cone and spread outward into the atmosphere, significantly impeding incoming sunlight. An unnatural mantle of darkness settled across most of the eastern Mediterranean region, extending as far away as northern Egypt, located some 400 miles (644 km) to the southeast. Meanwhile, immense displays of volcanic lightning flickered above Thera's now deserted fields and villages. In addition, as the explosive outbursts of debris from the cone reached their height, several monstrous blasts could be heard as ominous, distant thunderclaps by the peoples then inhabiting India in the east, Britain in the west, and central Africa in the south.

By the time the mighty eruption cycle had finally reached its peak, more than 7 cubic miles (29.2 km^3) of rocks, ash, and other debris had been expelled from Thera's huge magma chamber. For a few minutes, or at most a few hours, the vast mass of rock and soil contained in the island's midsection dangled unsupported above a miles-wide void. At last, the universal and inescapable will of gravity could be denied no longer. The towering cone, its foothills, and the island's other central sections plunged downward with a roar heard halfway around the planet. The force of the collapse unleashed an airborne shock wave identical to that of a nuclear bomb. Shooting outward in all directions, it crossed the nearly 80 miles (129 km) separating Thera and Crete in mere minutes and slammed into Amnisos and other coastal sites like a giant tornado. Any people who were standing outside unprotected were swept up into the air and smashed to death against buildings, trees, and other obstacles.

For the survivors, much worse was to come. At the same moment that the great shock wave hurried outward from ground

The massive eruption of Thera's volcano is shown in this lithograph. Many of Thera's residents had fled to nearby islands years earlier when smaller eruptions of the volcano began.

zero on Thera, the sea swiftly poured into the massive crater created by the collapse. So much water was displaced so quickly and with such tremendous force that an enormous surge of energy rippled outward through the surrounding waters.

That stupendous energy took the form of a tsunami traveling at hundreds of miles per hour. In the open reaches of the sea it was barely visible because most of the wave was contained within the deep water. But as the relentless submerged force neared the shallower waters along Crete's northern coast, it made those waters swell up into a frightening, onrushing liquid wall. Reaching a height of 150 feet (46 m) or more in some places, it raced inland, flattening many structures and partially demolishing even the largest and strongest. Because most of the Minoan palace-centers were situated a bit inland from the coasts, they suffered moderate to

In addition to hearing Mycenaean merchants tell about the disaster that had struck the Aegean region, the Egyptians may have themselves experienced some of the long-distance effects of that event. After all, the large waves that battered Crete and other nearby islands were not confined to the Aegean Sea. Evidence shows that, diminishing in size over time, the tsunamis struck all of the Mediterranean Sea's coasts, including those in northern Egypt. Also, some of the airborne ash would have caused darkened skies in the daytime as far away as southern Italy and northern Egypt. One Egyptian account, found in an inscription commissioned by the pharaoh Ahmose (reigned 1550–1525 BCE) actually appears to connect odd disturbances in northern Egypt with a disaster in the faraway Greek lands. The account states, in part,

> The gods expressed their discontent [by sending] a tempest [that] caused darkness in the [northern] region. The sky was unleashed, [sounding louder] than the roar of the crowd [and] houses and shelters were floating on the water [for] days. [The ocean] broke out and fell on our towns and villages in a great wave [and the main city of] the sea peoples [the Aegean-centered Greeks] went under the sea. Their land is no more.

Medinet Habu Inscriptions 37, 46, 80, 102, and 109, quoted in Jurgen Spanuth, *Atlantis of the North*. London: Sidgwick and Jackson, 1979, p. 175.

heavy damage. Simultaneously, the monster wave barreled across the Aegean and struck all of its coasts, drowning large numbers of people and destroying villages, towns, docks, and ships.

The Minoans in Decline

The Minoans had far more ships than any other people in the region, so their naval losses were the greatest. Whereas most of those vessels docked in ports were destroyed entirely, those few on the open sea received lighter damage. Under normal conditions, these losses might not have permanently crippled the Minoan economy. But the Theran disaster was so immense, and located so near the Minoan heartland, that many of the people who knew how to repair damaged ships or build new ones were killed.

As Cambridge University historian Oliver Rackham explains, "Certainly there would have been shipwrights and ship repairers who in the nature of their business would have lived within reach of the tsunami. The drowning of these men, and the loss of their special skills, might have been a disaster more permanent than any loss of ships or equipment."[43]

Archaeological evidence clearly shows that, despite the death of untold thousands, including many key craftspeople, enough Minoans survived the disaster to ensure that their culture would live on. There was at least a hope that over time they could rebuild and recoup their horrendous losses. It would be an uphill battle, to be sure. After all, many square miles of farmland had been rendered useless by the ashfall. The loss of most of the ships meant that reestablishing normal trade and the economy might take decades. The grim specter of death had likely visited every surviving household, causing extreme despair across a severely demoralized population.

If these had been the only difficulties the Minoans faced, subsequent history might have been very different. A resurgent Minoan empire might well have led Bronze Age Europe in directions that today can only be imagined. But as it turned out, the Theran calamity had set in motion a dilemma that spelled ultimate doom for Minoan civilization. While Crete and the other Minoan islands had borne the brunt of the volcanic cataclysm, the Greek mainland—outside of its few low-lying coastal areas—had emerged largely unscathed. It did not take the mainland Mycenaeans long to discover how badly the disaster had crippled their seafaring neighbors.

The subsequent takeover of Crete and the other Minoan strongholds by the Mycenaeans did not occur all at once. Evidence suggests that it happened in stages, over the course of decades or longer. Steadily, the surviving Minoan farmers and laborers became subservient to the mainlanders. New merchant ships were constructed over time, but when they began visiting foreign ports once again, after a long hiatus, the captains and chief traders were now Mycenaean rather than Minoan.

This transfer of power from islanders to mainlanders was known to and actually memorialized by the Egyptians. Modern excavators have found three revealing wall paintings in the tombs of some high Egyptian officials who lived during the middle of the second millennium BCE. These images show Cretan merchants, whom the Egyptians called Keftiu, carrying various luxury goods. In the first two paintings, the Keftiu wear Minoan-style kilts with wide slits, like those seen in Minoan wall paintings found at Knossos. The third painting, in contrast, depicts the merchants differently. Their outfits have been painted over to show kilts that wrap around the thighs, a style characteristic of Mycenaean culture. As J.V. Luce points out, this alteration in the tomb paintings "must surely have political significance. As such, it seems very good evidence for dynastic change at Knossos [after] the Theran eruption."[44]

In the Fullness of Time

During their initial visits to Egypt, the differently clothed Keftiu brought with them more than goods to trade. They also offered the Egyptians startling news that was destined to have a lasting significance for future Western societies. The Aegean traders told a colorful tale of a horrifying catastrophe that had recently rocked their home region. An entire island had sunk into the sea in a single day, they said, and it had crippled an advanced island civilization. Later, long after the Mycenaeans themselves declined and their merchants stopped visiting Egypt, Egyptian priests remembered that story, which continued to pass from one generation to the next. In the fullness of time, their distant descendants met an Athenian named Solon and passed on the tale to him. In turn, his own offspring kept the story alive until a later Athenian, Plato, wrote it down.

Did You Know?
For reasons still hotly debated by historians, Mycenaean civilization rapidly declined and collapsed between 1200 and 1100 BCE.

By Plato's time, memories of the Bronze Age kingdoms, rulers, and events had become garbled, inflated, and distorted into myths. No one could estimate how long it had been since a great civilization like the one he described as Atlantis had flourished in the area. This is not surprising, says University of Louisville scholar Robert B. Kebric: "The Greeks were notoriously lacking when it came to time-reckoning, geography, and their early history. Consequently, location, circumstances, and chronology often became confused, and details changed or became embellished, [so] stories could become so muddled over the centuries that it was impossible to ascertain the true circumstances of an event."[45]

Over the span of many centuries, folk memories of the once powerful and sophisticated Minoan civilization and its demise morphed into the fantastic tale of lost Atlantis. Perhaps no one has ever summed up this fateful process better than the very first scholar to notice the similarities between the real Minoans and mythical Atlanteans. In his now iconic 1909 article, K.T. Frost said,

> As a political and commercial force, [the Minoans] were swept away just when they seemed strongest and safest. It was as if the whole kingdom had sunk in the sea, as if the tale of Atlantis were true. The parallel is not fortuitous [accidental]. If the account of Atlantis be compared to the history of Crete and her relationship with Greece and Egypt, it seems almost certain that here we have an echo of the Minoans."[46]

SOURCE NOTES

Introduction: Atlantis Removed from Fiction's Realm

1. James W. Mavor Jr., *Voyage to Atlantis*. New York: Putnam, 1969, pp. 103, 112.
2. Mavor, *Voyage to Atlantis*, pp. 11–12.
3. Mavor, *Voyage to Atlantis*, p. 19.

Chapter One: The Global Search for Atlantis

4. Richard Ellis, *Imagining Atlantis*. New York: Random House, 2012, pp. 5–6.
5. J.V. Luce, *Lost Atlantis: New Light on an Old Legend*. New York: McGraw-Hill, 1970, p. 15.
6. Proclus, *The Commentaries of Proclus on the* Timaeus *of Plato*, vol. 1, trans. Thomas Taylor. London: privately printed, 1820, pp. 148–49.
7. L. Sprague de Camp, *Lost Continents: The Atlantis Theme in History, Science, and Literature*. New York: Dover, 1970, p. 20.
8. Ignatius Donnelly, *Atlantis: The Antediluvian World*. 1882. Reprint, Scotts Valley, CA: CreateSpace, 2016, p. 479.
9. Camp, *Lost Continents*, pp. 42–43.
10. Shirley Andrews, *Atlantis: Insights from a Lost Civilization.* St. Paul: Llewellyn, 2001, p. 241.
11. Mavor, *Voyage to Atlantis*, p. 11.

Chapter Two: The Minoan Connection Revealed

12. Mavor, *Voyage to Atlantis*, p. 63.
13. Spyridon Marinatos, "The Volcanic Destruction of Minoan Crete," *Antiquity*, vol. 13, 1939, pp. 429–30.
14. K.T. Frost, "The Lost Continent," *Times* (London), February 9, 1909, p. 3.
15. Plato, *Critias*, in *The Dialogues of Plato*, trans. Benjamin Jowett. Chicago: Encyclopedia Britannica, 1952, pp. 483–84.
16. Plato, *Critias*, p. 483.
17. Rodney Castleden, *Atlantis Destroyed*. New York: Routledge, 2001, pp. 138–39.
18. Charles Pellegrino, *Unearthing Atlantis: An Archaeological Odyssey*. Charleston, SC: Amazon Digital, 2017, p. 91. Kindle edition.

Chapter Three: Memories of Minoan Glories

19. Plato, *Critias*, p. 482.
20. Plato, *Critias*, p. 482.
21. Plato, *Critias*, p. 483.
22. Luce, *Lost Atlantis*, p. 183.
23. Plato, *Critias*, p. 484.
24. Plato, *Critias*, p. 484.
25. Frost, "The Lost Continent," p. 4.
26. Plato, *Critias*, p. 484.
27. Rodney Castleden, *Minoans: Life in Bronze Age Crete*. New York: Routledge, 2002, p. 21.
28. Plato, *Critias*, p. 479.
29. Castleden, *Atlantis Destroyed*, p. 6.
30. Plato, *Timaeus*, in *The Dialogues of Plato*, trans. Benjamin Jowett. Chicago: Encyclopedia Britannica, 1952, p. 446.

Chapter Four: A Blast That Shook the World

31. Mavor, *Voyage to Atlantis*, p. 112.

32. Mavor, *Voyage to Atlantis*, p. 113.
33. Marinatos, "The Volcanic Destruction of Minoan Crete," p. 426.
34. Luce, *Lost Atlantis*, pp. 83–84.
35. Spyridon Marinatos, "On the Atlantis Legend," *Cretica Chronica*, vol. 4, 1950, p. 210.
36. Hesiod, *Theogony*, in *Hesiod and Theognis*, trans. Dorothea Wender. New York: Penguin, 1973, pp. 50–51.
37. Quoted in Mavor, *Voyage to Atlantis*, p. 40.

Chapter Five: Atlantis's Last Days Revisited

38. Andrew Collins, "Where Was Atlantis?," Intrigue. http://intrigue.freeservers.com.
39. Quoted in Helen Velissaris, "Akrotiri's Link to Atlantis," *Neos Kosmos*, May 29, 2014. https://neoskosmos.com.
40. Castleden, *Atlantis Destroyed*, p. 19.
41. Castleden, *Atlantis Destroyed*, p. 22.
42. Mireia Movellán Luis, "Rise and Fall of the Mighty Minoans," *History Magazine*, January 31, 2018. www.nationalgeograpic.com.
43. Quoted in Pellegrino, *Unearthing Atlantis*, pp. 275–76.
44. Luce, *Lost Atlantis*, p. 143.
45. Robert B. Kebric, *Greek People*. Boston: McGraw-Hill, 2005, p. A-9.
46. Frost, "The Lost Continent," p. 5.

FOR FURTHER RESEARCH

Books

Ignatius Donnelly, *Atlantis: The Antediluvian World*. 1882. Reprint, Scotts Valley, CA: CreateSpace, 2016.

Gale Eaton, *A Story of Civilization in 50 Disasters: From the Minoan Volcano to Climate Change*. Thomaston, ME: Tilbury House, 2019.

Richard Ellis, *Imagining Atlantis*. New York: Random House, 2012.

Gabriel Glasman et al., *The Secrets of the World's Seas: Atlantis, the Legend of the Lost Continent*. New York: Cavendish Square, 2018.

Charles Pellegrino, *Unearthing Atlantis: An Archaeological Odyssey*. Charleston, SC: Amazon Digital, 2017. Kindle edition.

Stuart Webb, *Atlantis and Other Lost Worlds*. New York: Rosen, 2012.

Internet Sources

Willie Drye, "Atlantis," *National Geographic*, January 21, 2017. www.nationalgeographic.com.

Holly Hartman, "Atlantis: Myth or History?," Infoplease. www.infoplease.com.

Internet Classics Archive, "*Critias* by Plato," trans. Benjamin Jowett. http://classics.mit.edu.

Internet Classics Archive, "*Timaeus* by Plato," trans. Benjamin Jowett. http://classics.mit.edu.

Lee Krystek, "The Lost Continent: Atlantis," Museum of UnNatural Mystery, 2006. www.unmuseum.org.

Mireia Movellán Luis, "Rise and Fall of the Mighty Minoans," *History Magazine*, January 31, 2018. www.nationalgeographic.com.

PBS, "Sinking Atlantis: The Fall of the Minoans," *Secrets of the Dead*, May 13, 2008. http://www.pbs.org/wnet/secrets/the-fall -of-the-minoans/61/.

Helen Velissaris, "Akrotiri's Link to Atlantis," *Neos Kosmos*, May 29, 2014. https://neoskosmos.com.

Websites

Ancient History Encyclopedia (www.ancient.eu). This excellent site provides a handy overview of what is known about the Minoans in its "Minoan Civilization" entry. It contains numerous links to related information, along with pictures and maps.

Sacred Destinations (www.sacred-destinations.com). This site includes the short, information-filled article entitled "Ancient Akrotiri, Santorini," which describes the archaeological site of Akrotiri, the Minoan town discovered by Spyridon Marinatos in the 1960s.

INDEX

PICTURE CREDITS

Cover: Oliver Denker/Shutterstock.com

5: Maury Aaseng

8: serato/Shutterstock.com

13: Shutterstock.com

19: Re-creation of the palace of Knossos, Green, Harry (b.1920)/Private Collection/© Look and Learn/Bridgeman Images

25: cpaulfell/Shutterstock.com

28: Steve Estvanik/Shutterstock.com

31: Pecold/Shutterstock.com

36: Destruction of Atlantis, English School, (20th century)/Private Collection/© Look and Learn/Bridgeman Images

40: Tsunami following eruption of Krakatoa (color litho), McBride, Angus (1931–2007)/Private Collection/© Look and Learn/Bridgeman Images

46: Fresco depicting a ship procession from Akrotiri, Thera Island, Santorini, Greece, detail, a coastal town, Greek School, (16th century BC)/National Archaeological Museum, Athens, Greece/De Agostini Picture Library/ G. Nimatallah/Bridgeman Images

51: Oil painting of exodus across the Aegean Sea as Thera's cone erupts (color litho), Townsend, Lloyd K. Jr. (20th century)/National Geographic Creative/National Geographic Image Collection/Bridgeman Images